DRAWING FLORIDA'S

ELISSA THOMPSON

SIGHTS AND SYMBOLS

 Enslow Publishing
101 W. 23rd Street
Suite 240
New York, NY 10011
USA
enslow.com

Published in 2019 by Enslow Publishing, LLC.
101 W. 23rd Street, Suite 240, New York, NY 10011

Library of Congress Cataloging-in-Publication Data

Names: Thompson, Elissa, author.
Title: Drawing Florida's sights and symbols / Elissa Thompson.
Description: New York : Enslow Publishing, 2019. | Series: Drawing our
states| Includes bibliographical references and index. | Audience: Grades 2-5.
Identifiers: LCCN 2018007612| ISBN 9781978503175 (library bound) |
ISBN 9781978503168 (pbk.) | ISBN 9781978504776 (6 pack)
Subjects: LCSH: Florida—In art—Juvenile literature. | Emblems in
art—Juvenile literature. | Drawing—Technique—Juvenile literature.
Classification: LCC NC825.F59 T49 2019 | DDC 741.09759—dc23
LC record available at https://lccn.loc.gov/2018007612

Printed in the United States of America

To Our Readers: We have done our best to make sure all websites in this book
were active and appropriate when we went to press. However, the author and
the publisher have no control over and assume no liability for the material
available on those websites or on any websites they may link to. Any comments
or suggestions can be sent by email to customerservice@enslow.com.

Photo Credits: Cover and p. 1 inset illustration and interior
pages instructional illustrations by Laura Murawski.

Cover, p. 1 atsurkan/Shutterstock.com (photo); p. 6 Jose Antonio Perez/
Shutterstock.com; p. 9 Photo courtesy of HeliclineFineArt.com; p. 10
Creative Jen Designs/Shutterstock.com; p. 12 Atlaspix/Shutterstock.com;
p. 14 Yuriy Boyko/Shutterstock.com; p. 16 Terry Reimink/Shutterstock.com;
p. 18 Brian Lasenby/Shutterstock.com; p. 20 Scott Leslie/Minden Pictures/
Getty Images; p. 22 Julee75/Shutterstock.com; p. 24 Smith Collection/
Gado/Archive Photos/Getty Images; p. 26 Joseph Sohm/Shutterstock.
com; p. 28 Brazil Photo Press/CON/LatinContent Editorial/Getty Images.

CONTENTS

WORDS TO KNOW

coquina A limestone rock made out of seashells and coral.

French and Indian War The battles fought between 1754 and 1763 by American colonists, England, France, and Native Americans for control of North America.

keys Small, low islands.

peninsula A piece of land that sticks out into water from a larger body of land.

Seminole A tribe of Native American Indians who lived in Florida.

species A single kind of plant or animal.

subtropical An area that borders a tropical area.

zigzag A line, pattern, or course that moves in or has a series of short turns from one side to the other.

WELCOME TO FLORIDA

Oranges! Walt Disney World! And over a thousand miles of coastline—1,350 miles (2,170 kilometers)! These are the things Florida is most known for. Florida also has many lakes, rivers, springs, marshes, and creeks. The state's biggest industries include agriculture, banking, the space industry, and tourism. More than one hundred million people from all over the world visit Florida every year.

Florida used to be home to about two hundred thousand Native Americans called the Seminoles. The word "Seminole" is from the Spanish word *cimarrones*, which means "free people." These proud Native Americans were given this name because they resisted being made slaves by the Europeans.

The first Spanish explorers, including Juan Ponce de León, reached Florida's shores in 1513. Ponce de León claimed it for Spain and named it La Florida, "land of flowers." Around this time, Europeans believed that Florida was full of gold. In the late 1580s, English explorers like Sir Francis Drake came to Florida in search of wealth. Britain gained control over Florida in 1763, at the end of the French and Indian War.

Leatherback turtles, Florida panthers, and West Indian manatees can all be found in Florida's Everglades National Park.

Although ownership changed hands a few more times, future US president Andrew Jackson established a new American territory government in Florida in 1821. On March 3, 1845, Florida officially became the twenty-seventh state to join the United States.

Today, more than twenty million people live in Florida. It has the oldest population in the United States. More than one in five people living in Florida is over age sixty-five. Florida's capital city is Tallahassee, which has a population of about one hundred and ninety thousand people.

With this book, you can learn more about Florida's history and some of its key sights and symbols. The step-by-step instructions and guidelines in this book will show you what to do from there. The last step of most of the drawings is to add shading. You can add shading by tilting your pencil to the side and holding it with your index finger. Before you start, make sure you have all the supplies on hand and a clean, well-lit space where you can draw comfortably.

The supplies you need to draw Florida's sights and symbols are:

- A sketch pad
- An eraser
- A number 2 pencil
- A pencil sharpener

These are some of the shapes and drawing terms you need to know to draw Florida's sights and symbols:

- Shading
- Squiggle
- Teardrop
- Vertical line
- Wavy line
- 3-D box
- Almond shape
- Horizontal line
- Oval
- Rectangle

MEET PURVIS YOUNG

P urvis Young was a self-taught artist who was born in Miami, Florida, in 1943. Young never went to high school. He learned about art by going to the library and studying books about famous artists like Vincent Van Gogh and Rembrandt.

When Young was a child, his uncle encouraged him to draw, but he gave it up until he went to prison for two to three years as a teenager. While there, Young began to draw again. In 1972, he painted a large mural, called *Goodbread Alley*, on the plywood covering a row of empty houses.

Young painted what he saw around him, mostly his Miami neighborhood, Overton, which changed greatly when a highway was built through it in the 1960s. Many of Young's paintings show his neighborhood through the artist's eyes. Thanks to the popularity of his paintings, people began to visit Overton again to see his work.

Young used paint, ink, and collage materials like cardboard, book pages, phone bills, and more to create his pieces. He was famous for painting police cars, prison walls, and wild horses, among many other images.

Young's artwork often included trucks, trains, and tracks to show a way to connect from the inner city to the outside world.

Young died in 2010, at the age of sixty-seven. Today, he is still known for creating a great many paintings. You can find Young's art in museums around the country, including in Florida, Pennsylvania, Georgia, and Washington, DC. When you see his paintings, you can experience how he felt about his home for yourself.

Let's Draw a Peninsula: Map of Florida

The southernmost state in the United States, Florida is a peninsula that borders the Atlantic Ocean and the Gulf of Mexico. The state's major cities include Tallahassee, Miami, Jacksonville, Saint Petersburg, and Orlando. Florida borders

Alabama and Georgia. Florida has two national forests, Ocala and Apalachicola National Forests, and Everglades National Park. Lake Okeechobee, one of Florida's largest lakes, spills into the Florida Everglades 100 miles (161 km) away. A 150-mile-long (241 km) chain of islands off the coast of Miami makes up the Florida Keys.

- Tallahassee
- Castillo de San Marcos
- Magic Kingdom
- Cape Canaveral
- Everglades

1

Draw the angled shape as shown.

2

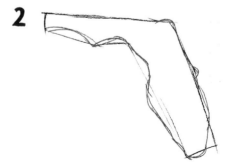

Add curves to the angled shape.

3

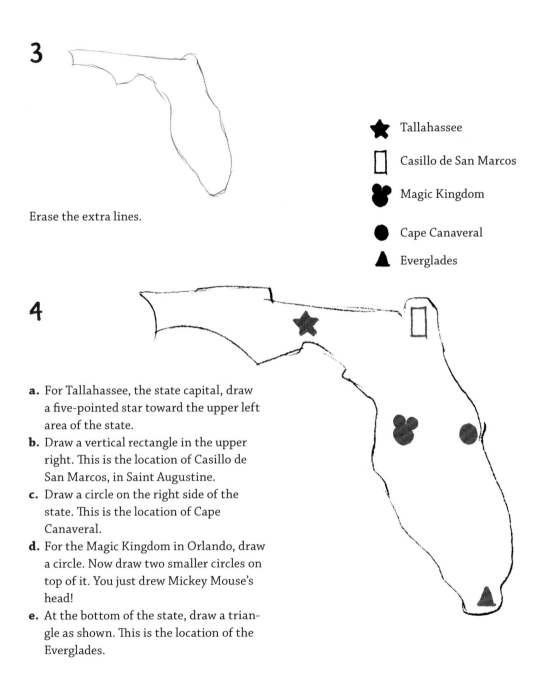

Erase the extra lines.

★ Tallahassee

▯ Casillo de San Marcos

🐭 Magic Kingdom

● Cape Canaveral

▲ Everglades

4

a. For Tallahassee, the state capital, draw a five-pointed star toward the upper left area of the state.

b. Draw a vertical rectangle in the upper right. This is the location of Casillo de San Marcos, in Saint Augustine.

c. Draw a circle on the right side of the state. This is the location of Cape Canaveral.

d. For the Magic Kingdom in Orlando, draw a circle. Now draw two smaller circles on top of it. You just drew Mickey Mouse's head!

e. At the bottom of the state, draw a triangle as shown. This is the location of the Everglades.

A Changing Tribute: The State Seal

In August 6, 1868, Florid adopted its state seal, but it looks different now. In 1970, the state legislature recommended some changes be made, which were completed in 1985. The tree in the seal was changed from a cocoa tree to a sabal palmetto palm, which became Florida's state tree in 1953. The words on the seal read "Great Seal of the State of Florida" and "In God We Trust," the state's motto. There is a Native American Seminole woman scattering flowers. Beyond her, sun rays beam out. In the background, a steamboat chugs by.

1

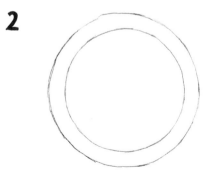

Draw a circle as shown. For neat circles, draw around a mug or a jar lid.

2

Draw a smaller circle within the first circle.

3

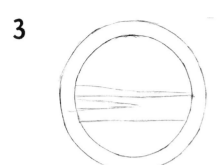

Lightly draw horizontal lines across the seal. This is the land.

4

Lightly draw the palm tree in the center of the seal as shown. Draw an oval on the bottom right. This is a bush.

5

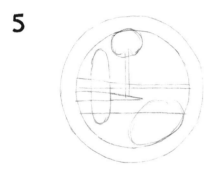

For the Native American Seminole woman, draw a long oval shape on the left area of the seal.

6

Lightly draw triangle shapes on the upper right area of the seal. This is the ship.

7

Now that all the main sections of the seal have been laid out, go back and add detail. Draw leaves on the palm tree and bushes.

8

Add details to the woman by drawing her head, arms, and feet. Draw circles for the blossoms that are in her arms and falling to the ground.

Native American Heritage: The State Flag

The Florida state flag has its seal in the center, featuring a Seminole woman. Approved in 1899, it is white with a red X. Seminoles were

Native Americans who lived in Florida before European settlers came to America. They call themselves the Unconquered People. The Seminole woman on the state flag and seal celebrates Florida's Native American heritage and the more than two thousand Seminoles who keep that heritage alive today.

1

Begin by drawing a rectangle. This is the basic shape of the flag. Use a ruler to make neat, straight lines.

2

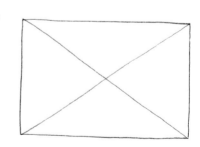

Lightly draw an X through the rectangle. This will guide you in the next two steps.

3

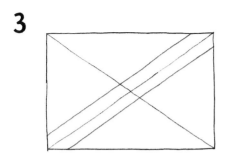

Go to the upper right corner and draw two parallel lines down to the left.

4

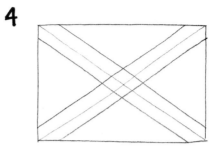

Now go to the upper left corner and draw two parallel lines down to the right.

5

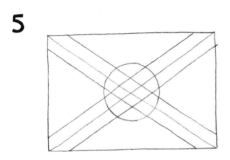

Draw a circle in the center as shown.

6

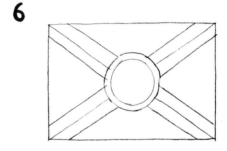

Erase the lines in the circle. Draw a smaller circle within the first circle.

7

Sketch the basic features of the state seal. Draw the Native American woman, the palm tree, the ship, and the bush as shown. You can go to the state seal chapter for help.

8

Color or shade in the X. You just drew Florida's state flag!

A Beautiful Transplant: The Orange Blossom

Florida's state flower, the orange blossom (*Citrus sinensis*) is not native to the state. Explorers most likely brought orange trees to Europe from Asia. From there, Europeans brought them to America. It became the

state flower in 1909. Orange blossoms grow on orange trees all over Florida. They have small white flowers with a beautiful and fragrant smell. Orange trees provide Florida with one of its most well-known products, oranges, and also the state beverage, orange juice!

1

To begin, draw a circle. This is the bud.

2

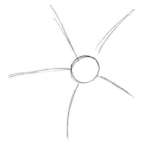

Draw five curved lines that fan out from the bud. These lines will help you draw the petals.

3

Use the curved lines as guides to draw the petals as shown.

4

Continue drawing the petals.

5

Toward the right side of the bud, draw a small circle. Draw another smaller circle within that circle.

6

Now draw more buds to the lower left of the flower. Draw three ovals and connect them to the flower with curved lines.

7

Behind the flower, draw four curved leaves that come to points. Lightly draw the lines inside the leaves. These are the leaves' veins.

8

Shade in the area around the bud and the tips of the petals.

Song Copycat: The Mockingbird

The mockingbird has a beautiful song—and it can copy the songs of other birds. The mockingbird became Florida's state bird in 1927.

There are ten similar looking but different species of mockingbirds. Males and females are the same size, about 10 inches (25 centimeters) tall. Mockingbirds are mostly gray with white underbellies and white markings on their tails and wings. The male and female live together in a nest made of grasses and twigs. Females lay three to six pale bluish green eggs with brown spots.

1

Draw an oval at an angle. This is the body of the bird.

2

Draw a circle on top of the oval. This is the head.

3

Draw lines that connect the head to the body. Extend the lines to draw the beak and tail as shown.

4

To draw the wing, make an upside-down teardrop shape on the body as shown.

5

Draw the legs and feet as shown.

6

Complete the feet. Add the claws by making little hooks. Draw the eye and extend the line from the beak under the eye as shown.

7

Draw the feathers on the wings as shown. You just drew a mockingbird!

Lustrous Large Leaves: The Sabal Palmetto Palm

Florida's state tree, the sabal palmetto palm, grows all over the state because it can thrive in many different types of soil. It became the state tree in 1953. It has a tall, thin trunk with no branches. Its grayish-brown bark looks smooth but is rough to the touch. The sabal palmetto palm has thick, leathery, fan-shaped green leaves that can be as large as 4–7 feet (1–2 meters) long. This palm bears black fruit that measures 3/8–1/2 inch (1–1.3 cm) wide and grows in clusters up to 7 feet (2 m) long.

1

Draw a tall, thin triangle shape at an angle. This is the trunk.

2

Turn your pencil on its side and lightly shade the upper part of the palm tree. This is the palm area.

3

Draw the palms by making hook shapes on top of the shaded area. Don't worry about making perfect palms.

4

Add details to the palm leaves by drawing lines that extend downward as shown.

5

Shade the areas between the palms. Draw in the lines on the trunk.

Everglades Resident: The Zebra Longwing Butterfly

Florida's state butterfly, the zebra longwing, is mostly black with yellow stripes. It became the state butterfly in 1996. These butterflies are commonly seen in Florida's Everglades National Park, the largest sub-

tropical wilderness in the continental United States. During the day, the zebra longwings fly slowly in a zig-zag fashion. Their favorite food is passion flower nectar. The zebra longwing stays with its family and rests in the same area each night. These butterflies sleep so soundly that if you pick up one slumbering butterfly, none of its family members will wake up!

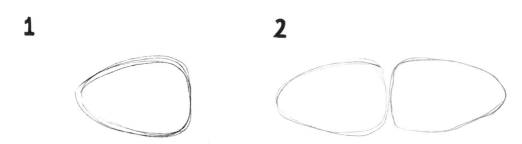

1

Draw the shape as shown. This is the butterfly's left wing.

2

Draw the same shape, but flipped, next to the first one. This is the butterfly's right wing.

3

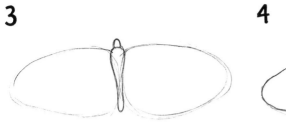

For the butterfly's body, draw the shape between the wings as shown. For the head, draw a small oval shape on top of the body.

4

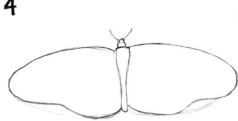

Draw antennae on top of the head. Draw a line across the middle of the head. Add detail to the bottom of the wings as shown.

5

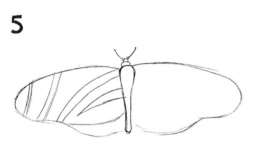

Add eyes to the head. Now draw the stripe design on the left wing of the butterfly.

6

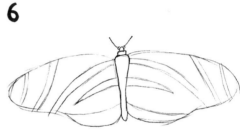

Carefully draw the zebra stripes on the right wing exactly as you did on the left wing.

7

Begin shading the left wing as shown.

8

Now shade the right wing and the body of the butterfly.

Protection Against Pirates: Castillo de San Marcos

Located in Saint Augustine, Florida, the Castillo de San Marcos was built by Spanish colonists for protection against pirates. Construction began in 1672 and ended in 1695. The fort was built with coquina, limestone rock made from seashells and coral. When the United States purchased Florida in 1821, the fort was renamed Fort Marion and used as a military

prison and storage facility. Some of the unique places to see in Castillo de San Marcos include guardrooms, watchtowers, and the gun deck.

1

Draw the square at an angle as shown. This is the center of the fort.

2

Draw another square outside the first square.

3

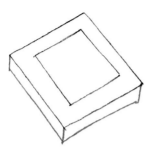

Connect the outer square with lines as shown. You just drew a 3-D box!

4

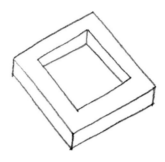

Connect the lines in the center of the squares as shown. Now you've added depth to the 3-D box.

5

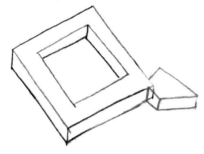

Draw the 3-D triangle shape on the bottom right corner as shown.

6

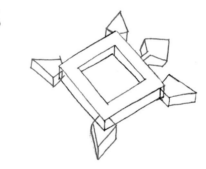

Before you start, carefully study the guide shapes. Now draw the 3-D triangle shapes on each of the corners. Draw an additional triangle shape in the center right. Notice how the shapes are different on each corner.

7

Lightly draw four lines that intersect the monument. Use them as a guide to draw around the fort, then erase them.

Two Buildings, History, and Progress: Florida's Capitol

Florida has two capitol buildings: an old one and a newer one, both in Tallahassee. In 1824, three log cabins served as the state's capitol building. The government grew, and a brick building was built in 1845.

In 1902, a dome and two wings were added. By 1911, government officials were working out of many different buildings. In 1972, money was granted to build a new capitol complex, completed in 1977. Today, government officials work in the new capitol building, and the old capitol building is the Department of State's Museum of Florida History.

1

2

Begin by drawing a long rectangle. This is the base of the capitol. A ruler will help you draw clean lines.

Divide the rectangle into three sections. The middle section should be slightly larger.

3

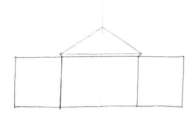

Slightly above the middle section, draw a triangle as shown. Now connect the triangle to the rectangle by drawing little angled lines.

4

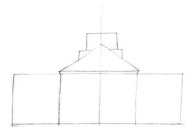

Draw a rectangle behind the triangle as shown. Erase any lines that cut across the triangle. Draw another rectangle on top of the first one. This is the base of the dome.

5

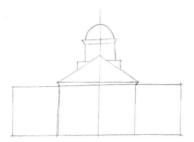

Slightly above the rectangle, draw a semi-circle for the dome. Draw a horizontal line underneath the dome. Now connect the dome to the rectangle with the angled lines.

6

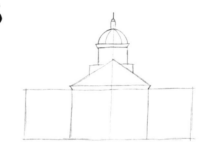

Add lines in the dome as shown. Draw the minidome on top of the first dome.

7

Draw vertical lines in the rectangle. These are the columns.

8

Draw more vertical and horizontal lines in the outer rectangles as shown. These are the windows of Florida's capitol building.

Family Fun: Walt Disney World Resort

More than twenty million people visit the Walt Disney World Resort in Orlando, Florida, each year. It is 43 square miles (111 sq km) and

boasts amazing theme parks, including Epcot, the Magic Kingdom, Disney's Hollywood Studios, and Disney's Animal Kingdom. There are also restaurants, golf courses, shops, rides, and shows to enter-

tain all day long, making it one of the top travel destinations for families in the United States.

1

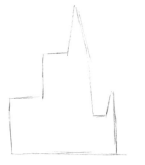

Draw the basic castle shape of the Magic Kingdom. Notice the two sharp points.

2

Start on the left side and draw the details of the castle as shown. Notice that the shapes on top are triangles.

3

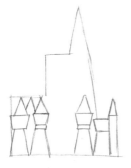

Now draw similar shapes on the right side as shown.

4

Draw a semicircle for the entrance. Above it, draw the pointed window and the details.

5

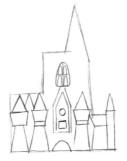

Draw more windows above the big triangle-shaped window you just drew.

6

Add more details of the castle.

7

Erase any extra lines. Draw the flags on top of the triangles as shown.

FACTS ABOUT FLORIDA

Statehood • March 3, 1845, 27th state
Area • 58,560 square miles (151,670 sq km)
Population • 20,612,439
Capital • Tallahassee, population, 190,894
Most Populated City • Jacksonville, population, 880,619
Industries • Agriculture, banking, space industry, tourism
Agriculture • Citrus, vegetables, field crops, nursery stock, cattle,
    dairy products
Animal • Panther
Band • Saint Johns River City Band
Butterfly • Zebra longwing butterfly
Wildflower • Coreopsis
Saltwater Fish • Sailfish
Song • "Swanee River"
Soil • Myakka fine sand
Gemstone • Moonstone
Saltwater Mammal • Porpoise
Marine Mammal • Manatee
Shell • Horse conch shell
Reptile • American alligator
Rock • Coral
Beverage • Orange juice

LEARN MORE

Books

Conklin, Wendy. *The Seminoles of Florida Culture, Customs and Conflict.* Huntington, CA: Teacher Created Materials, 2016.

Orr, Tamra B. *Florida.* New York, NY: Scholastic, 2018.

Waxman, Laura Hamilton. *Life in a Wetland.* New York, NY: Scholastic Blastoff! Readers, 2016.

Websites

Musuem of Florida History

http://www.museumoffloridahistory.com/education/index.cfm

There's lots to learn about Florida through these fun programs, like Florida History Day.

State of Florida: Kids

http://dos.myflorida.com/florida-facts/kids

This fact-filled website will teach you all about the state of Florida's history.

INDEX